KEEPING THE OUTLAW ALIVE

With thanks

KEEPING THE OUTLAW ALIVE

ALIVE

JARED SMITH

THE ERIE STREET PRESS

Some of the poems and essays in this collection
have been printed previously in literary magazines.
Jared Smith wishes to thank Menke Katz, William Packard,
Harry Smith, Thomas Fisher, and Quentin Howard for bringing
them to light in the following publications:

BITTERROOT MAGAZINE

"Autumn Is A Red Deer"

"If...But No"

THE NEW YORK QUARTERLY

"From the Rigging"

"Nobody Writes About Children"

"One"

"Face Of The Phoenix"

NEWSART

"The Incident"

THE SMITH and PULPSMITH

"An Evening In The Heartland"

"Entering"

"It Takes A Man"

"Keeping the Outlaw Alive"

WIND MAGAZINE

"A Day In August"

"Finding Love"

STAR-WEB PAPER

"Fast Food Lunch: NY"

© 1988 by Jared Smith
ISBN 0-942582-14-4

FIRST EDITION

PRINTED IN THE UNITED STATES

PHOTO: DEBORAH PARRIOTT

THE ERIE STREET PRESS
221 S. Clinton Avenue
Oak Park, Il. 60302-3113

KEEPING THE OUTLAW ALIVE--the title poem is a major chronicle
account of a seedy Odysseus figure, born 1852, dentist by
training, who drinks his two pints a day and is the speediest man
with a six gun in the west. This strong poem/saga, like all the
other good poems in this excellent collection, is about someone
who is restless and driven and haunted by all the furies of the
frontier.

Jared Smith wouldn't mind my saying he is a sort of surrealist
Edgar Lee Masters who is writing his own appalling annals of
America: ghost voices step forward and tell their modest stories
about how they've had to hack out their own survival because the
wild have to face the wild in this world. So the reader has the
curious sense that these poems are all quietly heroic, just as in
SPOON RIVER--although in Jared Smith's world the voices are also
ruthlessly satirical of our godforsaken materialism and its
satanic spinoff of murderous middle class values.

Instead of Walt Whitman's barbaric yawp sounding over the
rooftops, Jared Smith is practising a measured barf at the moon
which is utterly original and as solid as any poetry that is
being written today. It has a firm grasp of form, it has its own
unique music in line after line of low-key symbolist imagery, and
it is also austerely disrespectful of all the right things. I
like this poetry alot.

                                            William Packard

KEEPING THE OUTLAW ALIVE

From The Rigging

What discontent is it
that drove our early fathers
across the breadth of this continent
this wide wide continent in one hundred forty years?
Our early fathers who had our fathers' fathers as children
so soon who had the finest homes of their times
or who had at least like neighbors by their side,
so like the homes and white painted boards we come from
and women whom they strove to marry and who married
and who went with them in their discontent.
What is it made them carry the hammer,
the nails of sobriety west?
What discontent found our distant continent
and nailed sails upon it from the rigging of windblown ships?

Keeping The Outlaw Alive

Next time you're out in Tombstone
checking out the wood crosses on Boot Hill,
having a cigarette while looking over the museum houses,
smelling the stale Milwaukee beer of tourist traps,
noticing the dry green bushes that smell like
    Noxema skin cream
                    or
Are sitting on a green grass hill in Glenwood Springs
having a shot of red-eye,
feeling your lungs ache because the air's too thin
and you're plumping up your chest
thinking you're a long way from home,
    Have another drink.
Have two bottles.
And try to keep it straight,
because the civic tic-tac never did;
and a lot of people drowned in their blood
            maybe
for loving or hating the man buried at your feet.

In fact,
lie down. You have
been driving, John.
You're always driving.
You're on a holiday, recovering your breathing.
watch the land.
    Watch the clouds spinning their mist above you.
        Lie back, why don't you
            stop driving stop
              and lie.

            What
            do you say?

In rain I hear distance...
the clap of dead horses in mud
stirring drunken carcasses with the power of my name.
    That flattened glint of metal
so carefully removed
antiseptically
the soul that drives a man
removed
is apathetic hatred on these white sheets

           a shell
of burned powder
              You/Me yes
laid out by carresses pulses ladies in white
needing to protect the rainbow fantasy
   It's all colors all colors their white gown
our eyes caught in tight vibration.

                Yes,
                but

Any response is stronger
than sitting in a room in cotton baffles
trying to cage yourself from the mad
     Shooting them
Ripping the throat of someone weaker
          than them
instills fear
          in them
and the sorrow/the tearing in your throat
                better
than disavowal
you are here to feel

rain and the sensual flesh are here
outside newsprint carpets of plush venom,
remember,the tin badge Wyatt was filled with blood of others
                even brothers
and the ballads brought to children on their way to school...

                A red wall
follows my wall follows
along red the narrow guage canyon
     Progress
       is built into mountain granite
the gold dust air follows my lungs
blood on the country.
From the south this cell-cushioning roar,
this rotten stump fleeing brawls
its stained way to glacial lakes
     from swamp to desert to alpine stone
the shivered chairs, eroding bones of houses...

Talk. I am not thinking fast enough.
If a tooth of the law offend thee, rip it out,
as I have done my license is to draw out the rot
the pain flashed smooth with blood my hands
crabbed with the suction bag of life...

I am John Henry Holliday.

John Henry Holliday, DDS,
born in Valdosta, Georgia in 1852
in the like lifetime of Ike Clanton, Wyatt Earp,
William Bonner/Billy The Kid who killed one man
for each year he lived
to Civil War Georgia and Sherman's violent poverty
born nonetheless to books and dark suits
to studies in dentistry and
in 1872
to be told his diploma to practice was his epitaph,
that he would die within the year,
that his lungs breathed death into his patient's mouths...

I lie still unthinking/feeling metal bellows
a rusting steam engine wheezing mountains into its craw,
my back rigid the nervous fingers tapping cards into wood.
Moving my eyes in blood empty of oxygen burning my muscles.
If you look at the mirror the wrong way, friend,
it's easier for me to be the iron
sucking out that silver capsule that is you
than to ask your name.
They call me Doc and I drink two pints a day
            every day
and it doesn't itch as much as your wild thoughts
carry nothing beneath my belt...

            Yes,
            but

Watch him for a moment.
The bent man like a beardless Lincoln
riding his silver pocketwatch into your city
full of cloth leaves dancing autumn color,
opening an ever hungry business on the vaginas he carries
unopened in his saddlebags whole rivers the moon knows and you

have never walked,
closes them and disappears leaving only a blood
tainting the nostrils of giant rabbits grazing by the city hall.
Watch them for a moment
until they turn the mad hill darkness of their eyes upon your dreams...

Have you noticed how they gather
so tight into each other while you sleep
their fur is indistinguishable their ears a torn fury
rolling their sex sign across whatever shred of yourself escapes
the snapping of incisor jaws so large granite slabs across the hills
until you rise screaming there being nothing else
throw your arms around them yelling Here...

> Doc, you're tired and
> I can't follow you.
> Remember

Remember. I remember a darkness opening between mountains
where The Snake cuts obsidian from its banks
from darkness myself coming forth carrying a fishing pole,
laughing and coming toward me young
bigger than any mountain
burning
and raising that pole
until it became a rifle, its barrel
twisted with stars off inlaid metal and looming
down before me/
remember freezing until that anger shook me...

When I grew sand dust kicking
          (The green shrubs.)
          Soldier boots bright in their sword sing sun
     rivers of cotton moonlight,
my father who sang the southern locust
practiced spinnets in the parlor with
          My mother's fingers.
               an empty row of wooden boxes
               moving toward order
the European music of frontier gentility
smiling its faces in stories by the fire,
patchwork neighbors' children in the school of home...

And I had schooling,
oh, yes, Homer/math/reading a one
     room school
lucky beat it into me with a wooden board
until they burned Atlanta down
     rusting the silver wings
drove out my father's heart/my mother's life
became confederates in the Union camp
rode rails to politics
               to Mayordom from invested poverty asking why
               to Holliday Street all glitter in booming dust
               to Baltimore
  my blood congealing in my lungs
consuming the people in warehouse offices of trade,
oh, I had school;
I spit it back in nobility's mouths...

Mattie,
     I could not have you
  beyond that summer by the river.
But I went home from Baltimore a doctor to Valdosta.
     And it wasn't there.
And I went home.
     They said I had six months to live
     If I went west:
I cheated them/I played the cards,
the doctor of golden fillings for our solitude...

               But why are you telling this?
               This isn't what we'll
               write.

The only woman I lived with afterward,
I laid bare her skull with a .44
and took her till she couldn't walk
after she buried a bullet in the mattress
     by my head.
I took her square for four days
before she turned me to the sheriff in Tombstone
when he was looking up her dress.
And when I was acquitted
I paid her off and turned her out of town...

10

Gold Watch Holliday,
my grey suit the back wall of every saloon
from Dallas to Dodge to Santa Fe to Leadville,
the miners' gold my hands
swift and cold among the cowmen.
The order of the cards
the always search for law...

It was never winter in the dance halls
            train stars
                the trail
      the gas lamp housewife Biblereaders
    this   this is what I wanted
baking me biscuits.
      The cowboys different
killers of these as sand shifts hills.
But it was never cold
    in the dance halls,
their glitter heat in the smoke of distance,
 a turning of limbs on ice river mist...

                But what of the people
                and your time of law?

Virgil,
you remember
a blue star burned through his heart
which killed with the distance of the Union
which made nothing of night mountains
which implanted solidity
                No
No man ever saw me take my vest off
sand into wind
No man ever saw me mark the cards/
                                were terrified
each because there was nothing they could see
    of sun
dark tangled trails I never
killed a man
I the coldest temper a steel bough
feared by every cowboy
never killed for you Mattie was in my own mission
 all these years

like your habit flung across the prairie
too had that hollow maw that must be crammed
whole forests/rangers/whispers choked
                    into order
establishing the dead Valdosta...

                    You're going, Doctor
                    Holliday.

I always sat with my back to the wall,
my suit a cavern into flesh
or surrounded/melted
into Wyatt Virgil Morgan Ernest so that
no man ever knew where the scalpel flashed;
I was not trained to cut the flesh,
but the bony framework of a man's desire:
I, Doctor Holliday, Dr. Mardi Gras,
vision of a nightmare you cannot kill,
never killed a man without breathing
                    deep into his lungs
and then   slowly   for his mistakes
there was no turning back from me/
those California bounty hunters backing me
for the swifter cutting away,
the steal of life too fast,
dying in pool halls or on the trail
or growing old out on the coast.
Not me, the molder of metallic light.

                    But what do we cut on your stone,
                    Dr. Holliday?

Cut that I have known
both sides of every jail,
have taken the blows
from both sides of the jury box,
have lived in Baltimore and Denver,
have drunk two pints of whiskey every day,
and stood,
have planted bullets in every saloon
from Dallas to Leadville,
have squared off at twenty feet with guns blazing,
and stood,

12

and never killed a man with any gun I held.
And never took a bullet.
And stood...

Cut
that I knew Ike Clanton
and Johnny Ringo, who sang like death,
and stagecoach gunner Johnny Slaughter
and William F. Bonner, Billy The Kid;
that some of them were friends and some were not;
that all of them were afraid of me;
that I am only 25
and they are dead...

Cut
that I searched for order at cards
and made more money drunk than any sober man,
that I have cheated death through five years of death,
that I am the best dressed gunman of them all,
that I would not buy the law of books.
Tell them I killed a hundred men,
that I owned countless custom guns in velvet cases,
that I changed the history of the law in Tombstone
in exactly thirty seconds,
and they will listen...

Cut
that my woman, who lives
praying in an east coast nunnery,
is the only person I ever understood
and that only her life has kept me here
drawn into mountain cold liquor...

Cut
there is nothing more
important
than
keeping the outlaw alive...

                    "JOHN HENRY HOLLIDAY,DDS
                BORN VALDOSTA, GEORGIA, IN 1852
                GRADUATE OF BALTIMORE DENTAL
                SCHOOL IN 1872. AT THE AGE OF 20
            ONE OF THE GREAT GAMBLERS & THE SPEEDIEST
                MAN WITH A SIX GUN IN THE WEST.
            HE LOST HIS BIGGEST BET WHEN HE DIED
            NOV. 8, 1877, IN A GLENWOOD SPRINGS, COLORADO
            SANITARIUM WITH TUBERCULOSIS, INSTEAD OF
                BEING CUT DOWN BY A BULLET"

A Man Screaming

We carry knives and pistols
and rifles
Silver bullets too.
We're the boys from Camillus,
Who the fuck are you?

You go through the house and down to the basement
Inside there's another house--five rooms & a
bath hidden in the underground railway,
though you might expect two rooms from
outside. And you sit in the lower living room
looking out over the stereo with Muddy Waters
and old blues on it Taj Mahal, the room
strewn with antique furniture/bric-a-brac/
scattered piles of curling photographs dating
back twelve years and waiting to be
repressed having travelled to NY to Hawaii
and home some of them and others just
arrived from the black box and scattered
here remarkable photos in black and
white/in tints/in color of Jack Burger's
pate, of locks on the Bowery, of trees
and waterfalls, volcanos and bodies.
And you're looking out the window
over the stereo through a latticework
of still-dripping eight foot icicles
into a blizzard of flakes the size of
dusty millers settling on a summer. And
you're looking down a short and gentle
embankment of clean snow to an ice-over
canal filled with tree limbs and
beyond that a thirty foot wide rise and
then a trout stream clean with two
foot browns and rainbows. A wall-and-
maze of fifty foot saplings growing
along the banks and among them a
rusted cornpicker and busted silo
saying this was once growing land.
Beyond the stream a rapid rise

of white riddled
with naked trees. No fences. This
the first house almost built and in
the family for seventy years and
more. A wildness looking out into
the wild and laughing. What went

Fast Food Lunch: NY

I start by the docks where they take the Day Line out, the Circle Line, scows of refuse painted fast on a blue river backed by hilly white houses clear as pins on the far side. Tar painted timbers waiting for one-day vacationers, shaped into open rectangles around the memories of European trade, revolution's boots and the icy hunt for dead behemoths from the past. A steady stream of cars along the West Side Drive, but 42nd Street is naked at this end, only three quiet GM dreams passing me in the first long block. A cement school, I suppose it's a school--would someone bring their children to this desert on the edge of blue? No, probably a terminal surrounded by a chain link fence. Crates of boarded storefronts and bricked over windows on small buildings. A marine supply store and a blue--I kid you not--police station complete with two cruisers straight out of a child's construction set. This could be the memory of a watercolor dream.

On my right The Port Authority terminal, blank glass doors opening to descending stairs. Two young women are exiting, filled with the novelty of being lost. Flesh excited. The cavernous emptiness within those doors really is filled with the violence of open space you read about: the Minnesota girls hunting for fathers; the stolen handbag hustles; the bright fishbowls pushed out each night into the darkness of America.

The UN. Countries beat ploughshares into swords here with diplomatic immunity.

And the grand central. How can you have a departure or arrival terminal in the center of a city? It is a black hole, a drainpipe septic system sucking the city's flotsam into the ground each night and spewing them out still dazed each day.

The furs, the glamour halls, Paris dresses from France and Taiwan here closed in one time seamstress sweatshops, manacled between the gaudy sex shop signs, fast food stands Americanized from every corner of the world--does McDonald's really use 1/3 of America's potato crop?--and street swingers hunting for a place to be. The walkers here move faster, dancing around each other for the post position as they wait for lights. They are tall thin men, dark of many races and sleek sheathed younger women who do not understand where the limousines depart for Bermuda.

The Wall

Hey, Kim,
I tried to get by to see you today
eighteen years after you died.
After all these years remembering
how alike we were 24 years ago.
But it was raining and all I had was a suit
so I thought of how I might get over on a tour bus
anyway
and go with this girl who works for me
out to Arlington and maybe I'd find the black wall by chance
and maybe I'd find your name on it even though I knew the wall
wasn't there
and think it means something
beyond anything I know
to find your name among so many white marks.
But you see, we got to the tomb
of the unknown soldier
when I realized I had left papers that cost my company $32,000
unguarded at the Washington Hilton,
so wondering what it is to be dead, I
hopped a cab,
yelled at the driver
and returned...

      The papers gone
    disposed of by a bellboy.

I'm sorry, Kim,
I don't even know yet how to find the wall.
I should have said Take me to Vietnam
    to the driver.
I've got a wife and two young children
and have just sold my house
and I don't know where they'll live.
What is it like, Kim?

Sitting Dark In Life

I'm sitting dark in Chicago,
blinds drawn white
my apartment...
no
this wording is not right
because...
well, everywhere you go
despite the wording in advertisements
you or I take our own
everywhere we go
but Chicago is not New York
and the ladies dream
Chicago is a stevedore
shipping bulls to market,
ribbons, heavy trains in the wind...
outside my window.

So Far Descending

The soft things are not soft.
Perspective gives us this:
at 30,000 feet, descending, I laughed
and the lights, warm animals, warmed your thighs
so far down there where life is.

This Town Is Young

It is the grass growing
It is the universe of light years distant
   burned out
settling its dust on your car
Its oceans and love-wet women
dusting down from infinity
   on your car
     on your windows,

And as dark rises
she drops her skirt and sits
looking through plate glass
her dark hair up above her blouse,
leg-naked on fabriced seat looks out
then leaves in pirouette to the night
goes out to spread hot limbs on grass
spread eagled sticking her ass
in the face of city
recptacle

Come,
this town is sweet.

An Essay on Illuminations

The other day I spent an exhausting lunchhour looking at illuminated manuscripts in a museum that won't be named. (I don't like to name museums because despite being "non-profit", they and everyone in them earn far more than most of the artists of whatever genre who created the work that makes them fat.) In any case, as I was looking at the manuscripts, I wondered the blasphemous thought of why these works are considered as exceptional and rare as they are. Certainly, their creators for the most part lived the rarified poverty of Monkdom and never could or would have wanted to dream that the visions they went blind over would end up worshipped under glass. And then, too, these works, though beautiful and intricate, were all markedly similar to one another over the centuries their art was practiced.

Perhaps these gray meditations I was having were merely the product of a long telephone-choked day with a liberal dose of Tums thrown in. But I think not: the illuminations <u>are</u> very similar; and while some are technically more illuminated than others, they are none of them so beautiful in themselves that anyone attempts to duplicate the art today.

No, I think the worshipping of these manuscripts represents something far greater. I think the worshipping is for the man who devoted years of his life only to the intricate creation of these objects. It is a worshipping of there being something believed in which supercedes all other human drives. A worshipping of the quest as evidenced in attention to detail.

It's almost too bad that kind of worshipping is only evidenced through the distance of death and the study of ashes. That may be because no one will believe a man will die for something greater than himself until he has. In this, as in poverty, artists of any media and saints are one.

Of course, if artists and saints were worshipped too much, it would destroy their humility such as it is, their perspective and their work. How about if we just wonder or ask why they cannot be <u>liked</u> or respected for their attempts, even as Marvelous Marv Thronberry was for the early N.Y. Mets?

We die too soon and with too little beauty to entrust all our future generations to the word and data processors whom corporate America pays handsomely to push buttons. We value those processors too much; we know that because they are paid well. And payment, as every employee in a corporate system knows, is for perpetuating the power of the one who <u>assimilates</u> the data--not processes it.

So who assimilates now: surely not Katherine Gibbs with a megabyte memory; a silicon doctor who someone pays to put his life on wafers? No, because these activities use up all the time for assimilation. The artist, writer, builder on the bones and dreams of the living and the dead? Who pays the rent with what for what?

Impossibly A Businessman

I too am now impossibly strong in a non-exist world,
a purveyor of white frame house
dark windows solid in bone
and trees.
I the businessman/educator
walking in flowers blown forgotten
somehow where I cry a starved wolf
keening its teeth on a stone of tongue,
trees beating their limbs against the moon
steel rayed tracks of purveyance out across the heartland.
I have come here drawn by fear
that the ocean always pawing
might come
that the earth shifting its shoulders
might reach out
greedily cupping my hands before I have heard
before my children have been born to hear
crickets rolling in the wells of joy.
I who now know only man
or only I (or only eye) know
there might be some thing to stop this sting,
some suddeness the swan in all her
   beauteous stupidity
does not question of though even she believes in love
to the extent of holding to life for life.
I, the man, impossibly strong,
controlled control--oh, business of the gods--
go out here in the land of grain.

Give Our People

Give our people bread and onions to eat.
The onions should be large and pale as human flesh.
They should be dark as old blood.
The bread should be coarse
and sweet with the grinding of mortars.
It will dissolve their tongues.
Their tears will fill burning rivers;
their hands carve homes from the mountains.
We will live forever
as long as there are mountains.

THE MIND

        A JANGLED NEST OF WIRE.
WHAT THINGS COME HOME TO THIS???

If...But No

If I can draw myself into light
somewhere around sundown
in the midwest
a long way into clouds above
and into
fields of varying greens
I will be buried with the crops
to the music of crickets under moon.
If I can draw myself...
but that buzzing membrane scaffolding our wings,
we have too many eyes to feed!

This, Really, Is This

This is not poetry I can sing
This is the pressure of my blood being
crushed into tin cans by media
A poet, I am not
strong enough to sail against my culture
    forever,
I am but a boy. I have
children.
The sunset is beautiful.

When October Comes And The Wind Blows

38, with 3 children riding high school bicycles already,
they bought their first house
dreaming dying the American dream they
got a smallish house of white with a garage
knowing having fought nothing
comes easy to them though their sons sneer--
worked so hard seeding the lawn and
keeping the sprinklers going day
and night smiling to look young
like they had time to catch, they
trimmed everything to make it grow.

Anything that grew they trimmed
until it fit,
like words--even if they didn't know
what it was it fit
because it was shaped like every other tree or bush.
And mostly it did. Except the
tumbleweed
growing by nature by the driveway in spring
the year they moved in,
its leathery green leaf thongs
  a lost bit of something golden
they wanted to protect. It grew so well
so fast
so strongly wild
they trimmed it as a centerpiece/a
specimen
surprising them an upright young tree
perhaps
the only vertical in an otherwise horizontal green,
so they trimmed it
to look like a small pine tree
reaching toward some holy night outside their son's garage.

                              ✻

The mountains are, they know, cold animals
darting in at evening in circles
about the town,

given invisibility by rain shrouds or
morning mist or
smokestack high smoke technology.

Those mountains, it's a myth.
No one walks those mountains. No lights.
There are foxes breeding shadows from their eyes.

When my brother flew his iron bird,
pried open its fiery belly with plastic fingers,
the sun dragon suddenly rebelled,
tearing his arms until he pinwheeled down into the rocks.

I wish in telling you
I could erase him.

What Makes The Man Different

There are deer moving in the night of our blood,
sailing across hidden clearings,
eyes spread on the tongue of owls--whispering.

This is our clearing in the city,
where after five we can cross the streets no one knows
and breathe deeply until our flesh falls from its bone.

This is the field we believed others knew
because overgrown drives led that way--
not knowing their hard steel eyes waited only for us to turn,
to light from the stream filling these branches.

This is what makes us
an opening into the stars
and as distant as a stranger's hands.

The Wind In Winter

Cold wind rises,
        wanders in a circle,
touching on the nose of wolverine,
passing over his eyes,
      patting his ruff for something wild and free.
It moves south through the splayed legs of caribou.
When it leaves the north,
it is vibrating with the surprise of life.

As Evening Draws

The time is new--
    always now--
and I walk a meadow folded by evening
and by the untrimmed border of man.
    It is snowing
a distant coldness on my hand
my fingers spread palm upward
    crickets into their warmth.

The Company We Keep

On days when I can take a rest,
allowed by the company and, more particularly, by me
and the rest of the country is busy
trying to see if it can survive
itself
without me as we both know it must sometime,
I often climb hills surrounding home
and turning paths once laid down by richer men
or even abandoning them to lose myself myself
see
from the translucent frieze of vine
and tree growth I stumbled on by accident one time
how on looking down on concrete dreams of steel
they are mosaic starmaps, memories, pieces.
That they are islands quite as small
and isolated as the lost estates I walk,
though they are filled with men
and I with thought.

Evening In the Heartland

The couplings in life, the connecting forces, are uncertain and unsuspected as they pass. They are like a coal car rattling up a Colorado mountain pass on a dark night, where the desert montains bounce back an unseen confusion of metal rammed against itself. One never knows in the dark, which shapeless lump among the myriad is the critical piece which will tip the balance of life or its direction as a distant engine grinds itself into manmade echos.

Yet, all those lumps, or accretions of life do rustle and shift that way, constantly churning against themselves so that, even recognizing they are separate pieces or instances, they seem inseparable. The brightest instant is lost in the tumble almost before recognized, or worse, lies just beyond our grasp as our feet stumble toward it, only close enough to watch it covered over as the ground shifts again. Or, perhaps, we lift the desired moment once in a great while, and even then too often find that a new bend or direction has been brought about in our goals, so that this treasured moment is no longer relevant.

Our chances seem so remarkably small by now of finding anything. Yet, we carry on. What a remarkable genius man is in his survival, in his ability to look with amazement at even the darker rocks that will crush him when he falls, and to find mystery and hope in them.

Just to know, though! Just to know. Which instant of life even as you come upon it, is the one that will spin you on your way and swirl the other moments around itself in a giant maelstrom? Like the Socratic philosopher, we can only judge if we did the right thing by looking back on the shadows we created by the end of life. Like the Aristotelian, we hunt for patterns that are too large and make them simple so they will fit our understanding. Like you or me, we are, all of us, alive until the shifting stops and the pattern becomes terribly or beautifully clear to anyone who watches. Do not judge a man until he dies.

Whatever. Guessing in the dark is a crap shoot. Most of us lose and win at the same time because we don't see clearly enough to know, and because we're amiable enough to be adaptable and snuggle down like little puppies against whatever warm body comes along and calls itself god in our understanding. And then, of course, there are those of us who poise themselves by chance to spring from or to the right choice instant of life by chance, and spiral to jubilation. But even then on the blatently stupid assumption that their choices alone were the key and they were astute enough to see forever down the rails ahead.

There are very few of us who remain at ease with our situation throughout life. Discounting idiots, there are even fewer. Those who remain even materially comfortable are generally born to the highest-- and in this country, hidden--aristocracy. What can we do but be aware of these things? Perhaps this awareness can save our sanity, because something must if we are to remain alive and grow to understand why we carry these swollen bulbs of narcicism at the top of our spinal columns.

Again, there are very few of us. Neglect the media. Forget about the Yuppies and the overnight successes. They are born of someone else's need to tell a story around a campfire to make a living; nameless ghosts or numbers like the players on a baseball team that always numbers nine but has a great many more players in reserve to play the positions that must be played.

Autumn Is A Red Deer

Autumn is a red deer
bolting summer's trees behind it.
Autumn is the day of the year
she remembers him home.
Home from the sky and the black rivers.
Home from the static drop of water falling off eaves.
Just turning there as he was in sun
laughing easy one hand out to his son
then only three and growing
quickly between shadows.

Nobody Writes About Children

Nobody writes about children
  as if they were eyes rattling in pockets
following you and taking the world;
perhaps it is only because then
  you would have to admit it is given
in tiredness; in the day carried old,
gray on evening's feathers.

Nobody writes about children like
  they had children;
like the mystery between their legs
were colder than starlight
and followed them home then
thinking dresses flesh summer breasts
winnowing their teeth on night.

It Takes A Man

Noon noon
the corpses rose
rushed out dance tangle
   42nd street
 the middle town
joined hands clapped smiled
parted on into the gray
washed away each night
a coat a scent of death, when
a dog smells of that breath
 he dies within a day
the soap scent the soap the
proudest of our time in plastic tubes;
it takes a man to be a mockery of time.

It takes a man
to plant a flower on his land;
a seed to know the wind:
you too
your eyes the hollow moon
their distance
   is not this...
too soft the capsule of the shell,
your love
   your hate
too great to hold the smell of self. It takes
three letters to spell impossible.

Finding Love

Strawberries on the beach
at Rye.
My son is two.
He picks a stone from the sand
says Daddy rock water.
Turning takes my hand
carefully each foot slow toward
    the water
watching the large red berry ocean stone
 sand gulls sky wind wild noises
at once holding my hand.
Stops two thirds of the way
Says selectively More berry.
Waits until I too turn back,
then carefully over the sand again
and we sit upon the shore
eating the heavy red fruit of life.
Wind knocking tombstones across the sky.

A Day In August

A day like this I imagine
rolling through the nets of trees
crisping dew-spattered grasss
enfolds everywhere.
Your hurried lipstick tangled
in the trim nylons of communication
as out of place as the next block
the next city.

A day like this i walk the fields
bordering every bedroom in America
touched by the warm scent of idle flesh,
running your ashen limbs through my song
and choking on the small gray stones of memory.

The cellophane windows of locust shells
dissembling wind in packets
on the ground.

In Washington when they shot the president

the incident

This town is tired of you.
Maybe you are only riding in a taxicab
when the news hits.
They have shot the president.
They have shot the press.
They have shot the police.
They have shot the government.
The green lights are useless at George Washington.

This town pulls your entrails
into the black pit of 1963
where they first told you your color was wrong
so really wrong you could not listen
but merely tear your eyes out and
place them coast to coast of super highway
marking the thin edge of concrete death.

This town is tired
of your hungry crying.
It wants you to build fences and schoolyards
to shovel the blank sheet of winter off your memory,
to forget another precedent has died.
Whether you liked the thought or not
that it was there
and you were a part of it
with your pearl-handled rhetoric
and your easy ideas of god and television news.

This town is tired of you
because you raged at the cameramen
zooming on each spot of blood in dying color
and the urgency of canceling out
the sponsors' migraine aspirin commercials.

You'd best go.
Leave this town
before the plastic undertaker finds
you locked behind the walls of someone else's paycheck.
You'd better leave.
You'd better take your song and bury it.

Visions Of A Pencil

The man who makes the pencils
   that write the world
knows nothing but the dark blood running your veins.
Thoreau so tuned in a pencil
   packing plant picked six
      by hand
         each time
           for boxing
             for sale
the universal eye picking arrow
   heads from Massachusetts earth
    not stop too look
      but there
        and known
for the city man media man
            vacation/impressed
but didn't make them
  fill the gray American grain
    to the crushed limbs of trees
        America
the gray blank metal growing
      blank
the messages of madmen
the messages of numbers/proof
    of what
the semen stained night aria of art
        somewhere
in a paper cluttered factory
in moonlit aluminum dimestore windows
is waiting deafly for the breath
  of Man
blind as night on glass

Driving the Ashokan river
  in late summer

```
the peeled logs
            are frozen
in themselves the chute
      the spume
abandoned minesites in Colorado
            sage


        ----------------------------


What makes the draughtsman fly
            is lead.
```

Morning Owls

Mist rises from beneath fields,
from between the heavy legs of corporations
grazing across our finest,
chewing them up,
spitting them out
and moving on in search of life.
Call them a computer
or cells of the Oversoul
or grime encased machines...
they are the indifference
of blind owls staring into morning.

Exultance

As the plane flattens in its western rush,
I bend against its plastic windows curved,
my bones against its metal looking down,
to the red earth squares the checkerboard greens,
and I come inside the white paint homes,
the one in particular there beside the two-lane road
laid back about a quarter mile where a woman I can touch
fleetingly sits still thinking in painted walls
and feeling outward beyond beginning of memory.
And it is night.

There is no way
    through starlight
  no way as the television clicks
  no way as her bedroom light
a shadow of her combing her hair
  against meadow-lit curtain
she could know,
    or know either that I pass as well.

A blanket of rain soft cloud
is the floor,
and I above it.
So far above there is no touching
    wisp of wheels,
nothing but a genetic bone-sent memory:
the holes between the burning blank eyes above me close.

In the plane's turning on its wing
    I am sick exultant.
I too am lost beneath the stars.

A Response To a Conversation With William Packard Where We Tried To Define Poetic Craft As Practiced By All Schools Of Poets

words so tight
they outline the vulvas and cocks of your mind
like Calvin Klein ®cut-offs.

We are the Poets. We Live

We write about noise in the underground,
the dark slither of moonlight across gardens
leaving our saltless way among the bitter leaves of marigolds,
our trails staggered over seemingly harmless clods of earth
dipping drunken rolling among leaves or twigs unnoticed in day.

What magic mystery from our soft sides and bellies
left in the bedrooms of our visits to small towns!
We who feed on all things, for they look alike,
who curl in silence and bleed when touched by unknown hands,
yet move as slowly as the earth beneath oceans, as vast.
We who write about noise in the underground silently,
yet who scream and writhe at the salt of human tears.

Hibernation

The bear sharpens its claws
    on old tree roots,
sniffs spring coming in from Montana,
making an oily rag of its nose
slaps toward the potted palms
and moves through just
that suddenly
standing on a cream colored rug
hunched into your office silhouetted
by an urban landscape of glass.

Its eyes rheumy
play tricks on the pink lipped teeth.
It has come to say something
or for some reason deep in its gorge
tries to roll earth over your bones.
It feels beautiful in its heavy hair,
and lost in the synthetic light.

Beach At Oceanside

```
    you can tell                    waveflock
     age is not                    sand
something you are born                turning
with something the light spring      spreadeagled
     ing limbs                       the curled
LOOK                                          shells
    the heavy flesh               wings of scythes
beneath bikini legs                 into deepening sky
iron tanks beneath sun               a pin on the retina
oh, oh, the gravity            hanging where there is no
         age                             age
But the untalking moment of her sunset
sweeping her knees the groundless churning
               white of aqua
                 vita!
```

The Interview

I tell the newsman how
what she thinks to ask gets hooked
into a screen mesh on its way out,
but without mentioning the moths and katydids
reaching for us with sorrowful eyes on silk
waving their human legs.
She says to be specific.

Lady, I
don't think this has anything
to do with cunts or money,
I can feel in your bones
you are also
something scared and watchful
where it is raining,
Lady, I am trying to be specific
in ways your words are deaf to.

One

One evening, her tree pulled up roots
and hit the road for California, gathering squirrels
out there in the darkness where the highway branches.
She learned that trees too leave.

Her car was like this also
in that its sides were the color of autumn.
A child in the back seat waited for heart operations...
Sometimes he gave, but more often he received.
It was not better that he did.

She danced naked in the moonlight
spinning on one foot in the middle of Highway One.
The snow caught in her hair
breasts rubbed in neon.

Face Of The Phoenix

We are all shadows
and have been shadows
from before the first tree defining itself.

Shadows talk?
Does air passing before flame thicken?
Does the air heat creating wind
and does the flame itself thicken,
then feeding itself on the infinity of its distance,
for light in its travels is infinite.

We are all shadows
and have been shadows
from before the first skirl of water
laughing in the swirl of itself.

We take the word
and it is a thickening of shadow,
it is a passing in the shades of our lives;
We take the word and we are shadows
and the word becomes our shadows
and the word becomes art
because it is our pattern.

That is why we meet ourselves
in the word we call our history
and in the eyes of famous men we live in the shadow of
the young girls twirling down the streets
our songs
shadows
met and growing thicker in conflagration
as though feathers of ash
all of us shadows
are shadows on the face of the phoenix.

They've A Kind Of Patronage

For success go abroad, my bard,
Go to England or France or Rome.
But once you've been to England, my bard,
you can never never come home.

It's in England the people pray for the poets
and in France they dance at your feet.
In Greece they'll love you, though they'll forget,
and in Erin ye've a gilded seat.

But you'll never come home the man you went,
a man among men who can't pay the rent.
You'll never fight like Americans do,
and you'll write lousy limericks too.

So be a great poet, a writer well-read,
stay here where the pay won't go to your head;
remember what Hemingway might well have said,
with a hole in your mind you're just as well dead.

Model For A Romance

```
                  one man is s
                             u
                             r
       She is a trapeze act   r
                             o
                             u
                  reh gnidn
          with love
            in that


    trying to make her flesh
    greater than it is
    something to look toward
            always
            while
         one man
Another
          is also waiting
        toward her a dark vacuum
        and he will be the one
    who removes her viscera for the grave
```

The Eyes Too Walls

My skin, a loose cloth rolling
along glowing stone beneath sea, drinks
sober men exhausted to itself.
A locust rattles, blooms,
night a lightening flower crackling through its skull.
Skin covers all.
The eyes, too, left unstained,
empty now as hospital rooms,
beds changed and colorless walls repainted.

Evening Coming In The East

Nightwalker walks these valley nights
only alone when least known
after the barbecue/the day's work/the checks
    cashed/
comes jingling silences from silver belt,
long-striding comes loping red-eyed
antennaed-fingered dream, disturbs the valley.

He reminds you of the undone job,
tears the curtains from dark women's sides.
Chants light through steely teeth.
He leaves you pitted with islands
like the night of understanding.

Invisible

I lie down among invisible animals
  fill my pockets with their soft eyes
and watch night unroll itself,
rising between my slackened jaws
and pouring down tree-stunted canyons,
billowing around the heavy rust of trains,
encircling men
a vision a dozen panoramas I return to
of watching without body the broken flesh
    seeping its moonlight into dust;
of the hat kicked crooked
the leather jacket dead again
        shining
while our footsteps shuffle homage
in sacrosanct circles of ourselves.
Of how at any moment
I will have one last explanation
and striking out
sudden will miss
everything.

Commuting

eyes ride their steel cushions along night
never into but wide wide
short hair framing soft flesh
and the glaze at summer's end

We are the people
We are the hope America
We are the children
still soiling ourselves in empty cribs
We the violence
The paternal order stern
    as rudderless ships

In Memory of Strain

For a year after John Strain died
his family left his house unsold in weed,
and we got our courage up, going by
as we did each evening through the field,
our arms about each other's waists,
wondering what it would be like to wait
as ripening seeds behind the cutlery
for your lover to come home
tired and alone at the end of the day.
A child wants to grow
even if wanting to believe doesn't make it so.

And so it was one weekend we met there
whether from lust or on a dare
to climb through the kitchen window,
stumble to the parquet floor,
and hold each other by the hand in our uncertainty.
In truth, right then there wasn't much to see...
we went from room to room afraid
to climb the stairs, to open closets, but we did,
and talk as loudly as if this house were made...
well, for ghosts and nothing else but us.
So that when we had sex quickly, and we did,
it would seem that we were alone more than enough,
and in leaving we would grow
in believing what we feared did not make it so.

Except in raising that dust across those floors,
in having laid our bodies sweat upon those boards
in first hunger, we were unsure
that the man who died there might not still live
in the patterns of leaves shivering their lives
upon the walls or a light quick dancing,
perhaps the sun off a distant car's chrome passing
on a dusty road. How not knowing then we knew
that around us an unbearable brightness flew
that in its separation from our bones
had no basis, no majesty of being but mechanical self alone.

There in that twining light
built only of light and shadows and air
we felt an iron scaffolding of fear
and the promise of broken time
welded into the bones of night,
as if to be ourselves was in fact to hear
more than either of us could bear,
through lives neither planned nor felt
except in the mad moments of belief
that what we carried in our finest moments of grief
was in fact the pelt of some great animal
blanketing the universe with its pungent smell
and in its largeness being what we saw as small.

Perhaps that is why as we left
we moved so much more slowly than we went in, caught
winding our way to the foundations laid
by Strain for his garage, now fading where the dirt crept in;
and I buried my hands in the shattered masonry, not
in memory or any cheap respect for what was paid
nor in guilt for any missing moments,
but in sharing of that distant civilization
that leaves a man with only what he makes,
and locks him in
spinning beyond our words into his walls.

You Cannot Write A Poem

You cannot write a poem
that says I don't know.
You cannot write a poem
that says I'm not perceptive enough
to know what I am doing in your world
unless it can say my world is not yours
and I am doing in it what you cannot do
and doing it like wind on the face of a leaf
and you will have to take my word for it
unless you throw your family away
and your camels through needles' eyes:
That's a safe bet...we all
have our heavy camels sweating their burdens
through the miles.

You cannot write a poem
that talks of music
and cries.
You cannot write a poem
that breathes, and loves, that is cold,
that moans in its bed with nightmares
remembering what was said to it twenty years ago;
or that will sacrifice its life
to see your children through school:
you would not want it to
Would you
unless it could lead that stale breathing
from your own mind as easily
Would you?

You cannot write a poem
that answers anything
when nothing talks
and no one listens
you cannot write a poem
like a kid with an unstirred can of paint
dipping in his wooden stick to raise clouds of color

and shunning the opaque,
knowing you cannot write a poem,
being a part of the wordless clumps
clinging to your arm
and tearing themselves into liquidity
and being poetry
gone before you speak.

The Penitent Voyeur

As she looked then
walking between rows of tigerlily
her dress was blue her eyes green
as she looked across the chill
and still despite our words
echoing there it was not her.

Perhaps that is why I've always liked
the distant shots;
anonymous white of underthings bulging
to come forth anonymous of face
except the memory.

This eternal thing that haunts the young
that flutters from their husks with age
how often has looked out from foreign eyes
has pertly twitched some girl's hips
or driven a crushing fist before letting it lie.

Something I think wanders these streets
it forms as shelves for holding tubes of flesh
and sticks it tongue inside bringing us alive
so that if finding ourselves in time
the dream even then is good

From Your Flesh

You walk into my room
highway-dark car at your back
sunlight caught in a bird's throat
your scent caught in my throat
we touch something between us
gives
elastic moment
in your entering I cannot
remove the hands of textile workers
from your flesh.

For A Woman Dead In Grand Central

I watch her rise in the morning
tired from the warm sheets not wanting to rise
but warm with the need to provide for child and husband
to hunt for the lover she left folded in paperback books,
drawing half asleep from her blouse a pale blue from a darkened closet
drawing it about her shoulders unaware
buttoning it in the mirror while she sleeps,
and not knowinig
it not knowing because it is only cloth
but it should since it is so much a part of her
it is the last blouse she will ever draw from the dark,
was to be even when wound onto a loom by a machine in some
    automated warehouse
far in time from mountains of burlington vermont.

THE PAYCHECK

THE NUMBERS   GHOSTS
SWIRLING FROM BEDROOM WALLS,
HUNGRY CLOSETS
       NAMING CAVE NAMES

For My Daughter In Moonlight

You are small
    huddled over a star
      in a dark room
         warm with the scent of sleep.

I would like to roll myself
into the infinite vision of your hope,
to be the green fire
    encased beneath moonlit snow
      heavy as air on your limbs.

Greenwich

This is Greenwich, Connecticut;
This is the end of civilization;
This richest percapita of America
where sleep pays to lie down by death

This is the scene:
the houses some of them whole cities, stretching
down to trees holding somehow
the concrete road safe, or
squeezing it against Long Island Sound
twisting it so the car jumps
but only at what squeezes out between the trees
or at what eats away at them
from the other side.

This is the condominium
of the blonde daughters of computer czars
of the seltzer swigging sons of landscape gardeners.
This is where they dock the Honey Fitz,
President John F. Kennedy's yacht,
next to the Showboat Restaurant,
tying the sterling silver taste of lobster
to the tainted smell of something not quite sea
rolling through the leaves of dark.

This is the scene:
on the Showboat restaurant road--
and, yes, it is really there and
you are driving it in the night
between tree laden electric halos,
are talking to the silence sitting by you,
funneled between the partiers and trees--
you are suddenly at the opening of nothing;
at that precise instant where the road stops
and drops unwarning down into a night of stagnant ocean--
yes, here, just ten blocks from where I-95
plunged three cars through a bridge to death--
but this suddeness was planned
or forgotten
or the struggle lost the way a defeated wolf
will offer its throat to attacking teeth.

This is the scene:
where you get out and take two steps
to the jagged concrete edge,
where you feel the power of stone behind you
and your blood dances on two thousand years of western music
where you stare only into what you are,
where your skin opens only to the light of stars
where your skin goes cold to the sounds surrounding you
of night sucking its teeth along your shore
and the gurgle of fear through dry grass.

This is the place
civilization ends,
where the only roads are followed
by ships on invisible beams
where flesh goes down quickly
but floats on moonbeams up again
beyond the tearing of time.

This is the end of civilization,
and in turning back from it,
in staggering back to your metal case,
in hurling yourself against the brittle glass of nobility
in falling through into the showboat bar
you wonder why it takes money to live this way;
to literally live on the edge of death
    in style,
to picket-fence eternity for daytime dreams.
And how much would we know
if all men were allowed to live this way
or Greenwich crept outside its trees at night
and said
This is the end of civilization:
this broken, concrete street.

On The Official 40th Anniversary
Of The Dignitaries At The U.N.:

I wonder if it has ever done anything to save lives
of anyone except for making money for chessmen to buy chessmen.
The making of money is in a sense the saving
of lives
there is now little to see because of the glass waterfalls
where the river is the river looking at the river vertically,
except for the Dag Hammerskjold Stair and flagpole
and the Nelson Rockefeller Plaque--I think plague when I write this--
on this plot of rosebud anonymity of power.

I look out over the east river
beneath armed rooftops,
watching for some time a page of the wall street journal
slosh
a dying body fighting its last against the tides;
counting the unmarked fishing boats carrying rocket launchers this week.
Helicopters duck in and out among the buildings of Roosevelt
carrying dark tubes hunting shadows moving out of place against the sun.

I lean here in the open where generations of cattle died
twirling another helicopter in an arc above me above the people.
There are so many of us here with radios
binocularshifisetsnewspapersbookshotdogs with our friends
waiting for some news to come down the line.

Modern Man, Artificial Intelligence, And Humanity
A Short Essay

Each day it is harder for man to achieve a personal control over his environment as technology passes from speed of function superficiality. Where does the ego come down, if it is to remain in evidence at all? Is modern man becoming obsolete?

No, his computer is a weapon of materialism; placed together the factors of an immutably mutable world, discerning immediately the weakest points in the walls of inertia surrounding him. In other words, if you were not you but a component, it would find what block in the architectural structure confronting you would be the keystone, providing the greatest change if removed--perhaps causing the entire structure to collapse without intent. And your ego, needing recognition in itself in this world of buttons, demands that recognition. The button is pushed--by the component you: and the better your computer, the more complete the devastation of existing structure. The greater or more infamous your "instant name"--a distinction built only on change.

Because the computer does not know one vital set of elements you need as a human being to direct your destiny, to be a human being. It does not know you or your interior relationships with the universe... and so it does not know your capacity for change, whether when you breach the fortress of societal mediocrity it will be to slaughter the infidels within that fortress or to live among them in greater health.

There is no replacement for the mind, if only because it knows the body it is within and is responsible for. There is no substitute for disciplined training of that mind. There is the mind, and then a large chasm before the lucite blocks of clarity composing artificial intelligence.

JARED SMITH is the author of Song of The Blood: An Epic and Dark Wing: Book Two Of The Song Of The Blood. Better than 300 of his poems and essays have appeared in a number of literary journals over the past twelve years, and he has read his work and been interviewed several times on coast to coast Public Radio programs as well as having had a part of Song Of The Blood performed as a modern dance at Lincoln Center in New York. He has served in an editorial capacity for several publications and on the Board of Directors for The New York Quarterly. At 37, he resides in Illinois after having traveled extensively throughout the U.S.